Dear Mom

*what you've always wanted to thank
your mother for but never got around to saying*

Dear Mom

*what you've always wanted to thank
your mother for but never got around to saying*

Noah benShea

SOURCEBOOKS, INC.®
NAPERVILLE, ILLINOIS

Copyright © 2001 by Noah benShea
Cover design © 2001 by Sourcebooks, Inc.

Published by Sourcebooks, Inc.
P.O. Box 4410, Naperville, Illinois 60567-4410
(630) 961-3900
FAX: (630) 961-2168

Library of Congress Cataloging-in-Publication Data

BenShea, Noah
Dear Mom: what you've always wanted to thank your mother for but never got around to saying / by Noah benShea.
    p. cm.
  ISBN 1-57071-738-9 (alk. paper)
  1. Mother and child–Miscellanea. 2. Parent and adult child–Miscellanea. 3.
  Gratitude–Miscellanea. 4. Conduct of life–Miscellanea. I. Title.

HQ755.85 .B457 2001
306.874'3–dc21

                                                        00-066157

Printed and bound in Canada

FR 10 9 8 7 6 5 4 3

"The hand that rocks
the cradle rules the world."
—International Proverb

Dear Mom,

You and I have never had a problem talking. Maybe that's because you were always so willing to listen. Listening, you taught me, is a big part of talking. That's the kind of "mom lesson" we could all benefit from.

I am writing this letter to you, but it's not just for you. It's also for me. And it's also for a lot of other moms. Other moms who share with you the sisterhood that comes from giving birth, and giving, and giving, and giving.

I'm writing because I want to say not only out loud, but also in print, what needs to be said. I love you. And I'm proud of you. And I'm surely proud to be your child.

If that makes you feel good, good. It sure made me feel good to know that whenever I came home, you were there. There not to attack and question me—although you did ask more than a few questions—but there with a cup of tea, and love, and wanting to listen about how my day had been, how the night had gone. I can still see you sitting there at the old kitchen table in your bathrobe with your head resting in the palm of your hand. You would let me go on and on about where I was going to go in life or was afraid to go. And I thought you were the most wonderful woman in the world.

Over the years, I've made some of the journeys I once only dreamt of. I've seen much, including a great deal of my own blindness, and you know what? I still think you're the most wonderful woman in the world.

Love, you taught me, is an act of faith. And it was you who also taught me that when we lose our way in life and love, it is often because we first lose our faith.

One of my early memories was of a plaque you put up in our apartment. No matter how many times we moved, that sign was among the first things nailed to the wall. The message says as much about you as it has ever taught me: "It's nice to be important, but it's more important to be nice." I'm proud to be the student of the woman who taught me that.

What I learned from you is that we do not kiss our children so they will kiss us back, but so they will kiss their children, and their children's children. Still, here are some kisses for you, some "thanks to mom" with love, over time.

Noah

Dear Mom

Thanks for teaching me
how to make cookies.

And that moms are
tough cookies.

Dear Mom

Thanks for listening to my opinion and telling me that it's not unusual for eggs to think they are smarter than hens.

Dear Mom

Thanks for reminding me that
life is not always wonderful.
But it is an experience
filled with wonder.

Dear Mom

Thanks for showing
me that what others
see, moms feel.

Dear Mom

Thanks for reminding me that some moments you only meet once.

So be sure to make the meeting.

Dear Mom

Thank you for this prayer:

Dear God,
Don't show me what I can bear.

Amen.

Dear Mom

Thanks for taking me by the hand
and teaching me to cross the bridge
from sympathy to empathy.

Dear Mom

Thanks for showing me that what
makes a woman super is not
whether she breaks down
but how often she gets up.

Dear Mom

Thanks for reminding me
that visiting someone who is
sick will make me better.

Dear Mom

Thanks for teaching me that
hope is contagious and its
infection inspires.

Dear Mom

Thanks for letting me see that self-love is no more selfish than loving others is selfless.

Dear Mom

Thanks for reminding me to struggle with who I am but to keep an eye on who I might become.

Dear Mom

Thanks for making it clear to me that life is uncertain, and if I want a guarantee I should buy a vacuum cleaner.

Dear Mom

Thanks for teaching me that
when we're angry on the outside
it often means we're afraid on
the inside.

Dear Mom

Thanks for reminding me that
when we shut our eyes, the world
does not go into hiding.

Dear Mom

Thanks for showing me that there
is nothing we cannot grasp.

And nothing that cannot slip
between our fingers.

Dear Mom

Thanks for reminding me
that falling in love is very
different from landing.

Dear Mom

Thanks for teaching me that life
is a surprise party. And that
the invitations are in the mail.

Dear Mom

Thanks for showing me
that everyone matters.

And that the most glorious
bouquet is still a gathering
of single stems.

Dear Mom

Thanks for letting me see how
the truth is seldom hidden
but often overlooked.

Dear Mom

Thanks for reminding me that feelings are the facts of life.

Dear Mom

Thanks for this Life lesson:

Love to learn.

Learn to love.

Dear Mom

Thanks for reminding me
that emotions are oceans.

They come in waves.

Wash over us.

And wash away.

Dear Mom

Thanks for teaching me that feelings are sacred, but that doesn't mean we should worship our feelings.

Dear Mom

Thanks for reminding me that
everyone crying out isn't
crying out loud.

Dear Mom

Thanks for showing me that
sadness can be a smile that just
hasn't turned the next corner.

Dear Mom

Thanks for these Gardening lessons:

We all do a little gardening. Most of our problems are homegrown.

If you're looking for something to grow this season, grow more faithful.

Little grows big overnight, like little lies.

Rain is a reminder that heaven sometimes sends tears to water our garden.

Time is an orchard. Every moment is ripe with opportunity.

Dear Mom

Thanks for reminding me that
love is like perfume.

If you wear it, others will
get a whiff.

Dear Mom

Thanks for teaching me to see
that feeling for others is the
braille of life.

Dear Mom

Thanks for reminding me that
sometimes the only way to
keep from drowning is to
throw ourselves into the sea.

Dear Mom

Thanks for teaching me
that we are all sailors.

We all come down the birth canal
and are dropped into the sea of
anything is possible.

Dear Mom

Thanks for kissing me on my forehead and telling me it was the good fairies' secret sign so nothing bad could ever, ever happen to me.

Dear Mom

Thanks for reminding me that
laughing is sometimes
the best way to cry.

Dear Mom

Thanks for telling me that
love is a night-light.

And promising you'll
always leave it on.

Dear Mom

Thanks for reminding me that to
an oyster a pearl is a treasure
that began as a problem.

Dear Mom

Thanks for teaching me that too
many of us care more about
being right than doing right.

Dear Mom

Thanks for showing me
that what we can grasp is
often more important
than what we can grab.

Dear Mom

Thanks for reminding me that
sometimes we grow so comfortable
with our blindness that the
thought of seeing scares us.

Dear Mom

Thanks for these Cooking lessons:

Bake a smile. Nothing feeds
the soul like laughter.

Passion in life is like salsa. It doesn't
have to be hot to add flavor.

God's in the kitchen. Wake up and
smell the future.

Dear Mom

Thanks for showing me how with
just one finger we can touch life.
And be touched. And reminding
me to leave my fingerprint.

Dear Mom

Thanks for teaching me to welcome
the opportunity to embrace joy.
And to joy at the opportunity
to be embraced.

Dear Mom

Thanks for reminding me that
some of us will give our children
anything but ourselves.

Dear Mom

Thanks for showing me that mercy
is the courage to be caring when
it's comfortable to be angry.

Dear Mom

Thanks for reminding me that
we often appoint others
to disappoint us.

Dear Mom

Thanks for teaching me that caring is a goal we are no less for not reaching but much less for not chasing.

Dear Mom

Thanks for reminding me
that passions, like fashions,
have seasons.

Dear Mom

Thanks for letting me see that
those who are always right
are usually wrong.

Dear Mom

Thanks for showing me over time
how the hollow of sadness can
become the goblet of joy.

Dear Mom

Thanks for reminding me that
when two people discover
each other's blindness, it is
already growing light.

Dear Mom

Thanks for reminding me that while we
pray for what we want, God prays
that we will want for others.

Dear Mom

Thanks for showing me that faith is a
star wise men, and wise women,
still follow. And love is the
shepherd leading the way.

Dear Mom

Thanks for teaching me that manners are ritualized respect.

Dear Mom

Thanks for reminding me that we all
want to be both understood and
remain an inviting mystery.
And we will be both.

Dear Mom

Thanks for letting me see that the
people in my life are a bouquet.
And for reminding me to wake
up and smell the flowers.

Dear Mom

Thanks for taking the time to show me
that life delivers at its own pace.
And that patience is life's midwife.

Dear Mom

Thanks for these Prospecting lessons:

All that glitters is not gold.

All that it is gold does not glitter.

Dear Mom

Thanks for reminding me that what I
do for myself can also be positive
for something greater than me.

Dear Mom

Thanks for reminding me that how I make my bed in life is important because I'm going to have to lay in it.

Dear Mom

Thanks for teaching me that all self-empowerment begins with self-acceptance.

Dear Mom

Thanks for reminding me that
every heart has a door. And that
I should answer mine.

Dear Mom

Thanks for the reminder to be
patient because our plans
have plans for us.

Dear Mom

Thanks for the Zen lessons:

The empty hand is not empty;
it holds nothing.

No matter what you are thinking
about, remember it is only a quiet
pond that paints an honest picture.

Dear Mom

Thanks for these Economics lessons:

We all have different jobs,
but all work is sacred.

Looking at life and seeing little of
value can be very expensive.

If we don't pay attention, we pay later.
And pay more.

Dear Mom

Thanks for these Weather reports:

In everyone's life there are fear storms.
Faith flies in all weather.

Sometimes the only way to find our way
through blinding storms is with blind faith.

Our moments are like snowflakes.
They melt in front of our eyes.
And no two are exactly alike.

Life can be cold. Melt a moment with
someone you love.

This isn't the ice age, but too many of us are
still waiting to thaw. And blaming the weather.

Dear Mom

Thanks for showing me that good deeds are prayers' wings.

Dear Mom

Thanks for this reminder on
getting where I'm going:

Don't rush.

Mortality is a bus.

Everyone makes the bus.

Dear Mom

Thanks for the directions on how
to get anywhere more easily:

Catch life's current.

Hitch a ride.

Row with the flow.

Dear Mom

Thanks for letting me see that we're all gifted because we have all been given the gift of life.

Dear Mom

Thanks for reminding me that teaching
your kids to walk begins with teaching
them to stand on their own two feet.

Dear Mom

Thanks for the Health tip:

Gossip is poison given orally.

Dear Mom

Thanks for showing me that our
actions may only be drops in the sea,
but they send waves across time.

Dear Mom

Thanks for reminding me that
dreams are when our eyes
are wide-open shut.

Dear Mom

Thanks for teaching me that
the opposite of love is not
hate but indifference.

Dear Mom

Thanks for the lesson on Sinning:

Life is sacred.

What we miss in life is a sin.

Dear Mom

Thanks for teaching me that our
fears are as individual
as we are.

Dear Mom

Thanks for the History lesson:

History is often his story.
Or her story.

Dear Mom

Thanks for the travel tip:

**Wherever we stop on our journey,
the first person we meet is ourselves.**

Dear Mom

Thank you, thank you, thank you for this lesson:

Codependent sadness isn't caring.

Dear Mom

Thanks for these Lending
and Borrowing lessons:

Of all the things we can borrow
from each other, why borrow fears?

Of all the things we can lend one
another, why not lend strength?

Dear Mom

**Thanks for lending me the faith
to see that sometimes being
sensible doesn't make sense.**

Dear Mom

Thanks for showing me
that life is sweeter when
we're sweet on life.

Dear Mom

Thanks for reminding me that old
habits chain us to new habits.

Dear Mom

Thanks for reminding me that
when we observe the habits of
others as annoying, what we're
usually observing is our
habit of being annoyed.

Dear Mom

Thanks for the Exercise tip:

**Lifting spirits is a great
way to get in shape.**

And is good for your heart.

Dear Mom

Thanks for the reminder
that if we want to make a
difference, sometimes
what we don't do makes
all the difference.

Dear Mom

Thanks for the lesson on Hunger:

Any of us can feel full and still
be starving for affection.

Dear Mom

Thanks for showing me that
what we won't look at isn't
what we're blind to but is
our chosen blindness.

Dear Mom

Thanks for reminding me that
taking small steps can be a
great leap forward.

Dear Mom

Thanks for showing me that when
we offer others harbor, we
calm our own storms.

Dear Mom

Thanks for reminding me that
God smiled on us in the hope
that we would smile back.

Dear Mom

Thanks for the lesson on Courage:

Have the courage to
suffer happiness!

Dear Mom

Thank you. Thank you.
Thank you...

Moms are amazing gems.

They are as rare and precious
as they are common.

Dear Mom

Thanks for reminding me
that families are like quilts.

One generation is
stitched to the next.

Dear Mom

Thanks for teaching me that no matter
what I am cooking in life, caring
is the most important ingredient.

Dear Mom

Thanks for reminding me that a house
has to have a window and a door:

A door so we can come
into ourselves.

A window so we can
see beyond ourselves.

Dear Mom

Thanks for reminding me that
great things are often achieved
by those who never miss
the chance to do little things.

Dear Mom

Thanks for reminding me to
sweep the carpet but not to
sweep things under the carpet.

Dear Mom

Thanks for reminding me that sugar
makes food sweeter, but it is love
that makes life sweeter.

Dear Mom

Thanks for reminding me that
only people with bread complain
about not having butter.

Dear Mom

Thanks for listening to me when I had nothing to say and taking the time to talk with me even when you knew I wasn't listening.

About the Author

Noah benShea is an international bestselling author, philosopher, poet, scholar, and public speaker. In 1998, Noah gave an address titled "Toward a Caring Society" at the Library of Congress, to which the entire legislative branch of government and the diplomatic corps were invited. Throughout the past year, his activities have included a weekly radio show, a daily TV feature, celebrity author luncheons, and numerous speaking engagements. His previous books include *Jacob the Baker*, *Jacob's Journey*, and *Remember This My Children*.

Noah can be reached at www.noahswindow.com.

Also by Noah benShea

Dear Dad

*what you've always wanted to thank
your father for but never got around to saying*

Available in fine bookstores everywhere.